Simple
SMART
Skills

for teacher productivity
and learner engagement

Mike Palecek

SIMPLE SMART™ SKILLS

for teacher productivity and learner engagement

PUBLISHING HISTORY

Lulu Press trade paperback first edition –August 2008

ISBN-13: 978-4357-4398-4 (pbk.)

Contents

1

Mouse, Annotate and Capture

Think of your SMART Board™ interactive whiteboard as a giant touch screen for your computer. Instead of using your mouse and keyboard to control your computer, you are going to use the SMART Board interactive whiteboard in a much more tactile way for group learning and collaboration.

You can use your finger as a mouse on a SMART Board interactive whiteboard, by simply touching an object with your finger to select it. You tap twice or "double click" on it to manipulate it, just like you do with a computer mouse.

You already know how to use your favorite educationally appropriate websites and how to navigate through them to find the curricular content you want your class to use. Working with educational websites you already know is a great first step toward helping you and your students become successful SMART Board interactive whiteboard users.

When you annotate on a SMART Board interactive whiteboard, you are simply adding your own comments, diagrams and symbols on top of the image showing on the board. It is easy to do. Just pick up a stylus out of the pen tray (above) and write over any software image. Be careful not to use any regular pen or pencil, or any other sharp object as a writing tool on the interactive whiteboard interactive whiteboard. Sharp objects might damage your board.

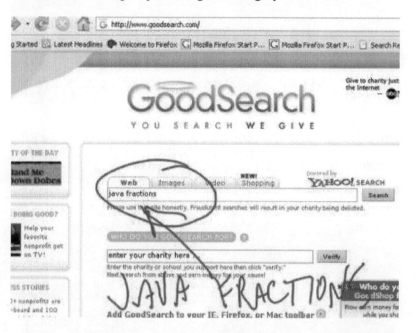

Annotate over a website to add interest, to help students focus, or to explain concepts in a more visual way. This helps students retain learning concepts better. On the image above, we are using a search engine called GoodSearch. (Your school can make money by encouraging students, staff and families to use GoodSearch. See the end of this chapter for details.)

When you are annotating on an interactive whiteboard, be sure to use firm pressure with your finger or stylus or the ink will "skip." If the lines are somewhat dashed, just press harder on the interactive board with your stylus or finger to create more pressure on the interactive board.

Many interactive whiteboards allow just one point of contact on the board surface. If you rest your hand on the board surface as you write, you will create multiple points of contact, making your writing scribbly. Hold your stylus as an extension of your hand. With just a little practice, it will be second nature for you to write on your interactive whiteboard.

Annotate to teach search strategies

The Internet is an amazing research tool. It is an unbelievably powerful research library at our fingertips. But students need instruction so they can find information in seconds, find appropriate information, and learn what to do with the information they find. An interactive whiteboard is a great tool to help them learn Internet use strategies. An interactive whiteboard is a great tool for giving an insightful lecture to prepare your class to do Internet research in the computer lab, library, or at home.

Transparency Mode using Notebook™ software 9

Digital Ink Layer using Notebook software 10

When you have opened up almost any software on your SMART Board interactive whiteboard (other than Notebook software and "Ink Aware" applications like Microsoft Word and Excel), and you pick up a stylus from the pen tray, four things happen. The screen freezes, a white band is displayed on the edges of your image, the cursor changes to a pen icon, and the SMART Floating Toolbar pops up. All these events tell you that you are in the "Transparency Mode" and can annotate.

This book is written from the point of view of you, the reader. We will walk you though actual techniques and lessons you can use with your own students. If you follow the instructions, your interactive whiteboard or computer screen should look like the screen shots below.

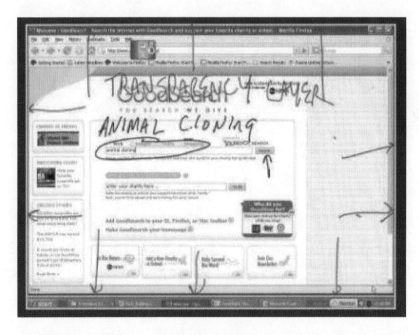

Because this book is not printed in color, we will describe the image above. You are at the GoodSearch search engine, you have picked up the blue stylus and written "Animal Cloning" on the screen. You have circled where your students should type their search criteria and have drawn a blue arrow under the Search button to start the search. In red, you have shown where the white rectangle is framing the screen to denote that you are in the transparency mode. If you put the stylus and eraser back in the pen tray, and touch the screen, the electronic ink will disappear. On the lower right corner of the screen a popup button will appear with the message "Click here to restore handwriting." After three seconds the popup button will disappear.

If you do not have time to click on that button, just pick up a pen from the pen tray, click the "Undo" button on the floating toolbar (shown here on the upper right) and you will return to the last action you performed on your SMART Board interactive whiteboard.

Imagine that you want your students to write a science report on Animal Cloning and it is one of the first times that you are using an interactive whiteboard. You can stand in front of your class, put your finger in the air and say, "I am going to use my finger as a mouse and double click on the (Internet Explorer)(Firefox)(Mozilla)(Safari) web browser icon on my computer to access the Internet."

"With the browser open, we can search the Internet. Let us go to one of my favorite search engines, www.GoodSearch.com. It is a great search engine which helps our school earn money every time any of us use it. But how do we get there?"

Pick up a pen from the SMART Board interactive whiteboard pen tray (you will see the pen tray sensor light turn red, denoting that you have selected a pen). Circle the URL and say "here is where we type in the website address, called the URL. "Does anyone know what URL means?" Then write U R L on the screen in blue.

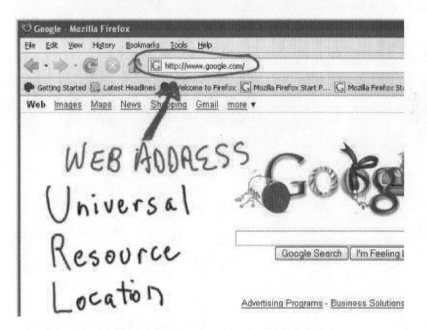

Wait a moment for a response. If you do not get one, in black, write Universal Resource Locator, and say "I think of it as a computer's nickname. It lets us easily find the site we are looking for."

In this example, you have changed pen colors three times. As you can see, using an interactive whiteboard to annotate, visually reinforces your verbal explanation, improving comprehension and recall.

Continuing your lecture, you say, "I could walk over to my keyboard to type in the URL, but we will do it from the interactive whiteboard. First, I will press on the virtual keyboard button on the pen tray." (On a 6 Series SMART Board interactive whiteboard it is the left button just below the eraser, with a keyboard icon on it). The virtual keyboard will pop up on the screen."

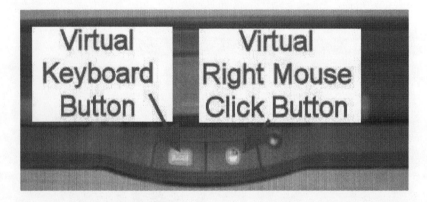

"Touching the top area of the keyboard, I can move the keyboard to wherever I want on the screen. I can then type out the URL on the virtual keyboard with my finger, so I do not have to take the time to go back to my computer keyboard to do it."

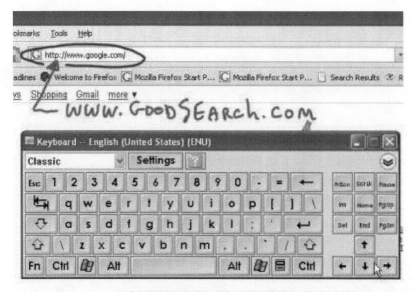

Above, Google's search engine is open, and you have circled the URL field in blue, written the URL you want in red, and clicked on the virtual keyboard to type in your search.

On a Windows PC, after the virtual keyboard pops up, highlight the text you want to replace, in this case, the URL www.goodsearch.com. Then press the arrow shaped Enter key (Mac users call it the Return key) on the virtual keyboard.

Continuing on, say to your students something like, "Your assignment is to write a 500 word paper on something of interest to you about animal cloning. What key words would you begin searching for in researching this paper?" Make sure you are annotating to add interest and reinforce concepts. This helps student understanding and recall. Pick up a stylus to write on the SMART interactive whiteboard with a color, or simply apply pressure to the SMART Board interactive whiteboard with your finger by selecting a tool and touching.

When you do a search for animal cloning, Michigan State University's site on cloning http://www.lib.msu.edu/skendall/cloning is sure to turn up. Below, we see an overview of the first page of the site, but let us explore it in more detail to see what more you can do with a SMART Board interactive whiteboard and the Internet.

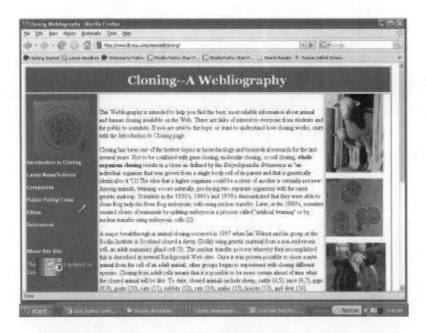

"Now," you say "let's go and take a look at a great cloning website: http://www.lib.msu.edu/skendall/cloning at Michigan State University. Here we see the first page of the cloning site. Let's explore it in more detail."

When you are using software other than Notebook software and you pick up a SMART Board interactive whiteboard pen, the Floating Toolbar appears. You can easily capture graphics from any software program and copy the graphics to Notebook software by using the SMART Screen Capture tool.

The easiest way to access this tool is to simply pick up a pen from the pen tray. The mini-Floating Toolbar pops up and you can use your finger as the mouse (when using the Floating Toolbar, do not put the stylus back in the pen tray). Click on the Screen Capture icon (shown at top left). Press on one corner of the image you want to capture and drag to the opposite corner. Then remove your finger from the SMART Board interactive whiteboard.

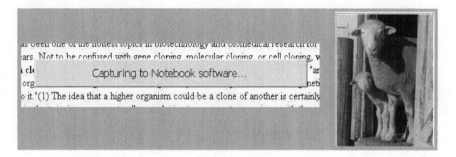

You will see the "Capturing to Notebook software…" message box and the cursor will change to an hourglass for a couple of seconds while the image is copied and pasted into your Notebook software file. If you have a Notebook software file open, the image will be pasted on the upper left corner of the existing page, or the upper left corner of a new page (depending upon how you have set the Screen Capture tool settings). If you do not have a Notebook software file open, your computer will open up Notebook software, create one page and paste the image into that page.

If you hold down on the interactive whiteboard and do not drag your finger, the entire viewable page (full screen) will be captured. If you make a mistake and do not keep pressure on the board while you are dragging, only a small cropped image will be captured.

You can also access the Screen Capture Tool in Notebook software. You have more control over the Screen Capture if you access it from Notebook software, then go to any other software that you want to capture.

The Screen Capture Tool works with virtually any software, not just websites. So, for example, if you want to capture screen shots of your favorite mathematics simulation program, SMART's Screen Capture Tool is one way you can do it. (Our favorite screen capture tool is the Import function of Corel's Paint Shop Pro drawing program, because it lets us take timed screen shots, to crop, accurately resize and much more from Paint Shop Pro. Paint Shop Pro was used extensively for the graphics in this book.)

Once you have clicked on the Screen Capture Tool, do not click on the blue popup tool box until you want to capture images. Navigate to the software you want to capture via the Windows Task Tray at the bottom of your screen, or open up new software. Get ready to do your work, and then select the capture tool you wish to use.

You can easily capture multiple images, because once a captured image is copied and pasted into Notebook software, the Capture Tool will continue to pop up, until you click on the red X close box. You can also minimize the Capture Tool and it will go into the Windows Task Tray until you click on it to use it.

If you want to capture multiple images to one Notebook software page, click on the checkbox in front of "Capture to new page." Then when you capture, you will pile up multiple images on top of one another in the upper left corner of a single Notebook software page. This checkbox controls how the capture tools in the Floating Toolbar operate.

Here you have selected the Area Screen Capture tool by clicking on the icon once, then lifting your hand off the board. Then you press on one corner of the image you want to capture and push and drag to an opposing corner. Lift off the board to capture the area you defined.

Mouse, Annotate and Capture

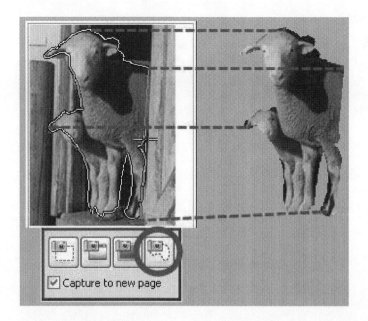

In the screen shot above, you have selected the Irregular Screen Capture tool by clicking on the icon once, then lifting your hand off the board. Then you have pressed on one edge point of image you want to capture and pushed and dragged, tracing around the image. This tool works like a lasso in drawing programs you may have used. If you do not reconnect your beginning and end point, this tool will connect the beginning and end points with a straight line to finish off the irregular capture.

Hint: if there is a straight line in the drawing (like the barn door frame in this picture), you might want to start your tracing there. Start at the spot where the back of the big sheep contacts the door frame, trace around, and finish up where the belly of the sheep is in contact with the door frame. Lift off the board to capture the area you defined.

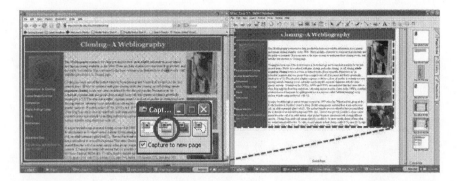

The Region Capture Tool captures a framed region. Click on this tool, press on the SMART Board interactive whiteboard, then move your finger around while constantly applying pressure to the board. You will see the different regions of the screen. In the above example, the website is in one frame, and the browser (above, with the URL address and menu commands) is in another frame.

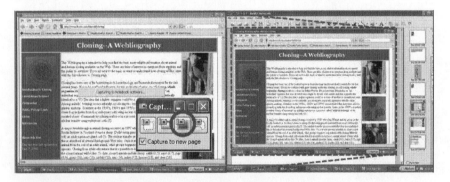

The Full Screen Capture Tool captures everything you see on your screen. Simply click on the tool as shown above.

Summary: In this chapter, you used a SMART Board interactive whiteboard to annotate over websites to add interest and reinforce learning concepts. You learned to use SMART's Virtual Keyboard to enter text into your computer while working on your SMART Board interactive whiteboard. You may have also learned some useful

Internet search strategies and how GoodSearch.com can be useful fundraising tool for your school.

The scoop on GoodSearch: *You may not know it, but the people who run search engines earn money every time you click on links to many of the commercial websites they list. The GoodSearch search engine gives 50% of its profits to non-profit organizations, including schools.*

Register at http://www.goodsearch.com/AddCharity.aspx *for your school or other non-profit organization to earn money at GoodSearch. Publicize GoodSearch usage in your school newsletters. When someone goes to GoodSearch to do a search, they type in the name of your school. The school earns about one cent for every search. It adds up. If a school has 1,000 people using GoodSearch, twice a day, in a year, the school earns about $7,300. Learn all about GoodSearch at:* http://www.goodsearch.com/About.aspx#faq

2

Simple Notetaking

My first grade teacher was very artistic and over the weekend would come to school and sketch detailed color drawings on the chalkboard. On Monday, she would introduce the concepts in the drawing to us and during the week, we would write over her beautiful drawings. After a few days, the drawings would be finished and we would erase them and clean the chalkboard.

Those drawings took a lot of time to do. With an interactive whiteboard, that teacher could have saved a lot of time. Research shows that one immediate benefits of using a SMART Board interactive whiteboard is the ability to quickly insert a pre-built graphic into a Notebook software file and to reuse previously created text and graphics.

Notebook software offers almost endless creative possibilities. But since this book focuses on simple, easy to do SMART skills, we are going to start by creating a simple lecture using Notebook software.

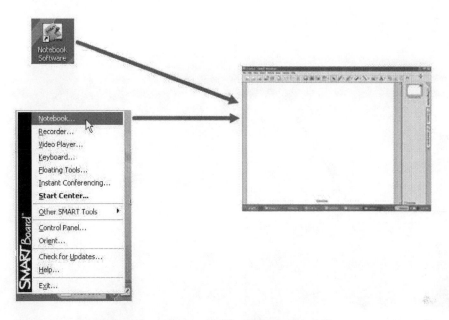

Starting up Notebook software 9 (for Windows OS)

As with many software programs, there are several ways to open a new Notebook software file. You can touch on the Notebook software shortcut icon on your computer desktop, or touch the SMART Board interactive whiteboard icon in the Task Bar. The SMART Board interactive whiteboard software menu pops up. Drag to select Notebook software, then release. If your computer does not have SMART software installed as a Start Up application, go to the Start Menu (usually in the lower left corner of the screen), go to All Programs, point to SMART Board Software, and drag to Notebook software.

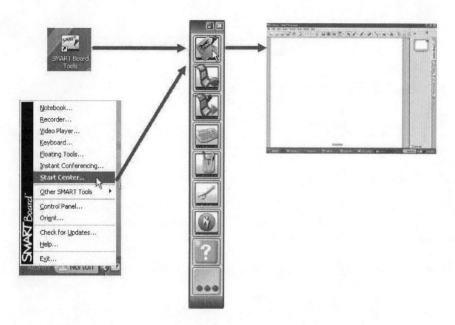

Notebook software 9 Start Center (for Windows OS)

Another way to open a new file is to click on the SMART Board Tools shortcut icon on your computer desktop, or click on the SMART Board icon in the Task Bar. The SMART Board software menu will pop up. Drag to select Start Center and release. This opens up the Start Center Menu Strip. Touch on the top icon to launch Notebook software.

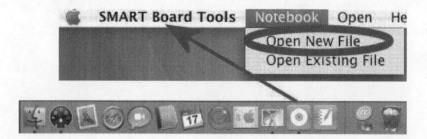

Macintosh users, click on the SMART Board tools in Notebook 10, which opens up Notebook and other SMART tools (under Open pull

---

Simple Notetaking

down menu). In prior versions of Notebook software for the Macintosh, this was the most common way to open up a Notebook file (or access any SMART Board tools).

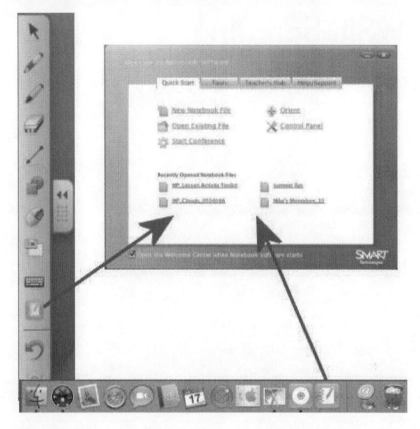

Notebook software 10 Welcome Cente r(for Windows and Macintosh OS)

In Notebook 10 software, click on the Notebook icon either in the the Floating Toolbars or on the Macintosh dock (or Windows taskbar) to start up Notebook software. You will go to the Notebook Software Welcome Center (shown above). If you click off the "Open the Welcome Center..." checkbox on the lower left corner, you will proceed to a blank Notebook file.

Shown above are the major regions of Notebook software 9: Tools Area, Whiteboarding Area and Special Area. The Tools and Special area can be moved to opposite sides of the screen. Different versions of Notebook software have different tool icons and the Special area may look a little different, but usage concepts are very similar in every version of Notebook software. The Special area includes the Page Sorter, Gallery and Attachment tabs. In Notebook software 10 the tabs have icons instead of text and there is a fourth tab titled "Properties."

To start writing notes, simply pick up a stylus from the pen tray and write in the Notebook software whiteboarding area. You can insert a picture by clicking on the Insert pull down menu at the top of the screen. To do this, select Picture File... (Insert -> Picture File...) You can also click on the Gallery tab in the "special" area and either double click or click and drag a picture to the whiteboarding area.

Alternatively, you can use the Screen Capture tool shown in Chapter 1 and capture an image from any software program.

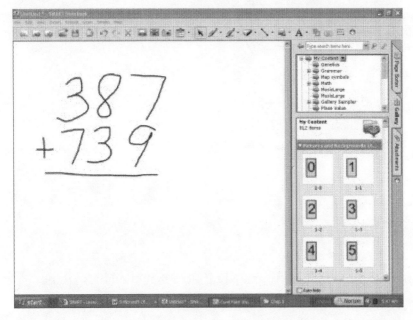

Above, we have just picked up the black stylus from the pen tray and written this addition problem. At the top of the Notebook software file, we touched on the "Full Screen" icon (blue rectangle with four white arrows pointing to the outside corners) to go into the Full Screen mode.

Notebook software Full Screen Icon (on right side of toolbar)

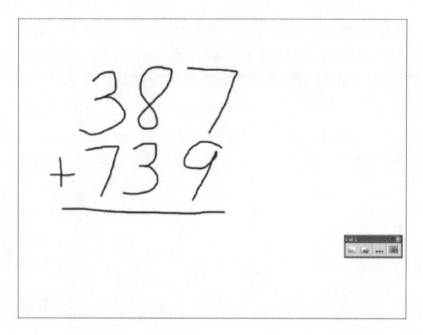

Going into Notebook software's Full Screen mode hides all the distractors, like the pull down menus, icons and Special navigation area. This helps students focus on your lecture content.

The Full Screen mode also makes the images larger and easier for students at the back of the classroom to read. The Navigational Toolbar pops up (on lower right) so you can go forward or back a page, access some other tools (three dots), or switch out of the full screen mode.

If you click on the "Go Forward" button (it is a icon of a page with the green right arrow) and you are at the last page, Notebook software will create a new page for your annotations.

Once you have finished your lecture, you can save it as a Notebook software file and reuse it again, by clicking on the Disk (Save) icon at the top left of the screen, or by using the pull down menu, File->Save.

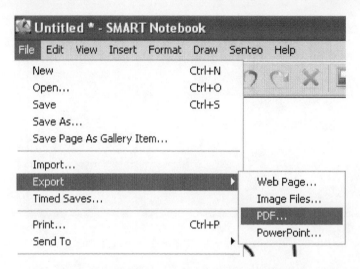

You can also export your notes to PDF, a very handy tool! Pull down on the File menu to Export->PDF. Adobe's Portable Document File is "the Rosetta Stone" of documentation. Almost every computer can read PDFs with Adobe's free Acrobat Reader software, which is pre-installed on almost all computers.

If you want to email lecture notes to an absent student or post notes to your website, PDF is a great format use for saving files. Because the PDF is smaller than the original file, it cannot be easily modified and the student almost surely can open it on her or his home computer.

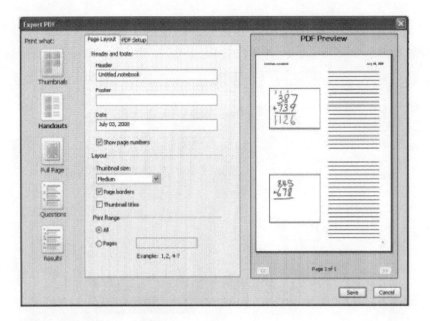

This is the Export PDF screen. On the left, you choose the format you want to save to (You will not use the Questions and Results options unless you have Senteo™ interactive response system software installed on your computer).

Here, we are saving our notes as Handouts, Medium Thumbnail size. You will see a page preview on the left side, showing what the PDF looks like. The handout format is popular, because students have room to make notes.

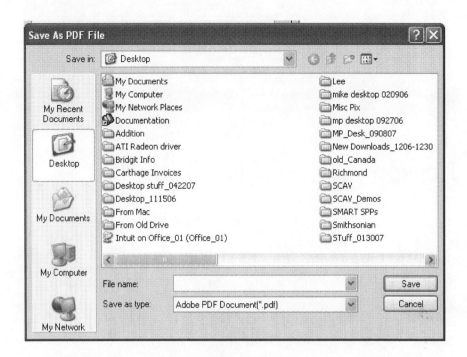

Finally, you will get a dialog box asking you where you want to save your PDF. Navigate to the location where you want to save the file. Then, touch on the Save button and the PDF is quickly created and saved.

You can do much much more with Notebook software. Because this book's focus is to give you SMART Board interactive whiteboard skills you can use right away, we will move to the Lesson Activity Toolkit. To learn more about Notebook software, visit the Training section of SMART's website and download the Printed Windows or Macintosh Quick Reference Guides and watch the Two Minute Tutorials at: http://smarttech.com/trainingcenter. You might also enjoy reading Simple SMART™ Skills: Volume 2 – Mastering Notebook 10.

3

Lesson Activity Toolkit

Research indicates that during the first two years of interactive whiteboard use, teachers work harder, as they build content to use with their interactive whiteboards. But there are many easy ways to integrate existing classroom activities with the interactive whiteboard.

One of the best tools available is SMART's Lesson Activity Toolkit (LAT,) introduced as beta software in Fall 2007, with the full LAT available as a free download in April 2007. What is nice about the LAT is that it is so easy to use, and you do not have to be an expert on Notebook software to utilize it. The LAT is great for reinforcing curricular content.

The LAT consists of "do-it-yourself" educational Flash interactive lesson "Activities": category sort, keyword match, multiple choice, note reveal, sentence arrange, tiles, timeline reveal, and vortex sort.

The Lesson Activity Toolkit has other goodies. "Games" include anagrams, crossword, hot spots, Sudoku, word biz and word guess. "Tools" include balloon pop, checker tool, dice–image, dice–keyword, question flipper, question flipper – image, random image tool, random number generator, random text tool, scrolling text banner, vote tool and word generator. Lots of good stuff!

The "Graphics" area in LAT contains over 500 items to help you make the Notebook software files you create look great. Included are navigation buttons, pull tabs and more.

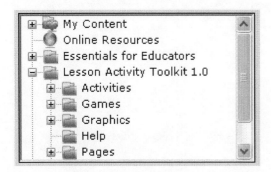

To download the Lesson Activity Toolkit, go to:

http://education.smarttech.com/ste/en-US/Ed+Resource/Software+Resources/toolkit/download.htm

The LAT installs as a Gallery in Notebook software. You must be using at least Notebook software 9.5 service pack 5 (Windows 2000 or later) or Notebook software 9.7 (Macintosh 10.4 or higher) for the LAT to operate. Adobe Flash Player 8 must also be installed on your computer.

Activities – common elements

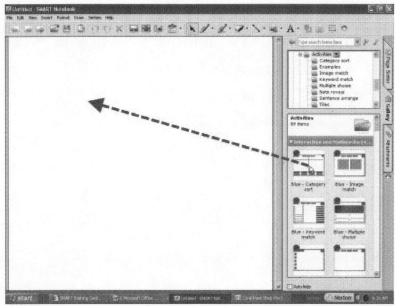

The LAT Activities are all Flash animations (the small red encircled F indicates it is a Flash file.) Drag an Activity from the LAT Activity folder to the Whiteboarding area.

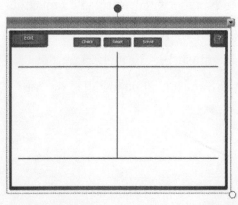

Touch on the medium blue bar at the top to drag it into position, the drop-down object menu (upper right triangle) to lock in place (Locking-> Lock in Place) or the white circular Resize Handle (lower

---

right) to resize. Click on the Edit button (upper left) to enter
information.

The top section of each LAT Activity includes an OK button on
the left to exit the edit mode. You can also enter a password here and
your work cannot be tampered with.

Depending on the activity, the top center section may contain
spaces for you to enter information.

At top right, you can choose your reinforcers - "Good Work or Try
Again," or the green (correct) checkmark and red (wrong) X. Click on
the round "radio button" to the right of the reinforcer you wish to use.

Choices that appear at the far top right vary depending on LAT
Activity. Here we is where you select two or three columns of
information to work with by clicking on the appropriate radio button.
You can also choose whether to have the Solve button show. Touch
on its check box.

Activities are available in blue, green, orange, purple and red
(different color frames and manipulatives.)

If you are a Macintosh user, avoid putting multiple flash items on
any one Notebook software page, because it can slow down the
animations. Sometimes when using Flash animations and Notebook
software, there is"gray box" residue on the Notebook software page
after using the Flash animation.

Activities - Category Sort

The LAT Category Sort object lets you enter up to 17 answers, in three categories. Facts we will use for the Category Sort:

<u>Animals</u>

Heterotrophic (do not make own food)

Mobile

Have tissue

Sexually reproduce

<u>Plants</u>

Make own food

Do not move

Cell walls

Asexual reproduction

Information source:
http://www.biology4kids.com/files/invert_main.html

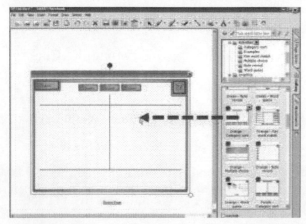

Start with a new, blank Notebook software file (File->Sort), then click on the Gallery Tab, click the + in front of the Lesson Activity Toolkit folder, and scroll down to the Activities folder. Click on the Activities folder, and in the Search Results box, scroll down until you find the gold Category Sort.

Drag the Category Sort object into the Whiteboarding area. Enter student directions or other information as you desire. Then click on the gold Edit button on the upper left corner of the Category Sort object to enter questions and answers. The screen shown below, appears.

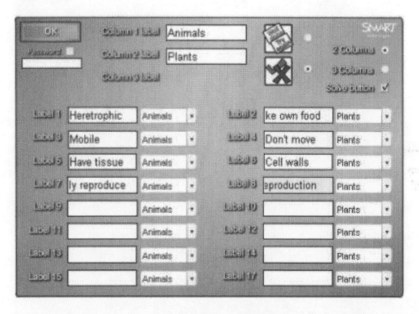

Enter the two category names as we have. The Category Sort object will immediately populate the answer pull downs (on right) with the correct answer choices. Enter the labels (you do not need to enter all 17) then choose the pull down answers for each item. On the right, choose the reinforcer you want to use, enter a teacher password on the upper left if you desire, then click the OK button in the upper left corner.

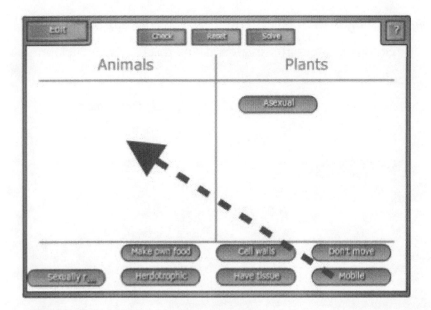

Running Category Sort, the student is now dragging "Mobile" to the Animals category.

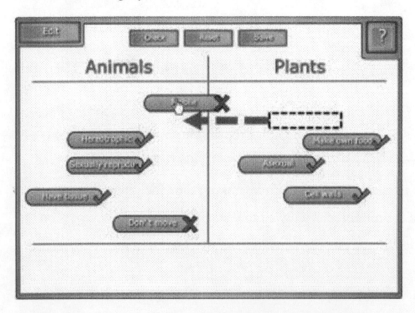

When all of the items have been dragged to categories, just click on the Check button at the top of the Category Sort object to check your work. Items marked wrong can now be dragged to the correct category, and the red X will turn into a green check.

Use category sort to review lecture points. Just remember, you need two or three categories and up to 17 items, and just a couple minutes of advance preparation. If you use more than 8 items, some answer buttons will be stacked on top of each other. If the label is too long to display properly, the text will show "…" in the label button. Just click on the label to see the full text.

When you click Reset, it re-sorts the items, so this is a good activity to play several times in class for students who need additional reinforcement. One idea is to assign students the task of creating a Category Sort as homework, then play the student created Category Sort files in class.

Activities - Keyword Match

The LAT Category Sort object lets you enter a group of five terms and descriptions. Facts for this Keyword Match example:

Invertebrates – none have backbones
Sponges – most basic invertebrates
Echinoderms – spiny skinned starfish, urchins, sea cucumbers
Anemones - central body and dozens of tentacles
Corals - hard skeleton of calcium carbonate

Information source:

http://www.biology4kids.com/files/invert_main.html

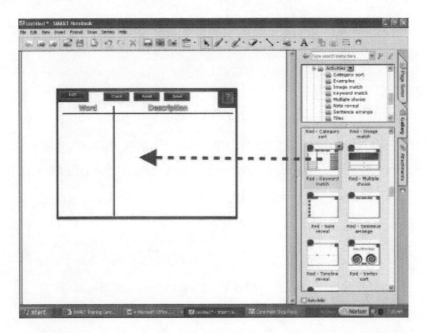

Start with a new, blank Notebook software file (File->New), then click on the Gallery Tab, click the + in front of the Lesson Activity Toolkit folder, and scroll down to the Activities folder. Click on the Activities folder, and in the Search Results box, scroll down until you find the red Keyword Match.

Drag the Keyword Match object into the Whiteboarding area. Enter other text as you desire. Click on the red Edit button on the upper left corner of the Keyword Match object, to enter terms and descriptions.

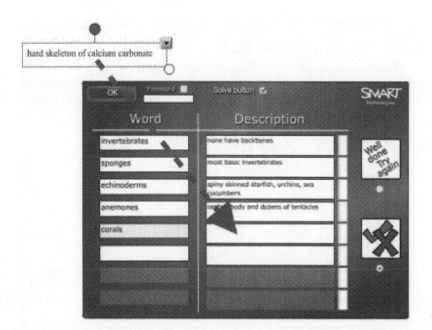

Enter the word and up to a two-line description for each of up to eight items. You can even copy text from a word processing program (or any other software) and paste it into Notebook software, then drag that text to an information field in the Activity. You can also hand write on your SMART Board interactive whiteboard, convert the handwriting to text, and then drag it into the information field.

Click on the reinforcer radio button you wish to use, then click the OK button in the upper left corner. Remember to save your Notebook software file when you have finished creating it.

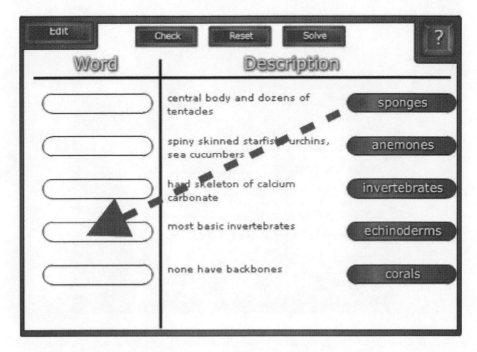

When you use the activity in class, have students drag the word ovals on the right side of the screen to the appropriate empty ovals on the left side. Note that the order of the word ovals has been scrambled. The descriptions stay in the order you entered them.

Reinforcers are shown after the work is done and the student selects the red Check box on the top of the Key Word Search object. The student can click Solve if he or she cannot figure out the answers and wants the answers revealed. Click Reset to clear the words and rescramble them.

Activities - Multiple Choice

The LAT Multiple Choice object lets you enter up to ten questions, with four (A-D) short phrase (two or three word) answers. We will work from this multiple choice test on the planets:

1. (B) – The planet closest to the sun is… A. Mars, B. Mercury, C. Earth, D. Venus

2. (D) – Used to be a planet, is now a "dwarf planet" A. Saturn, B. Uranus, C. Neptune, D. Pluto

3. (A) – The largest planet is… A. Jupiter, B. Earth, C. Saturn, D. Neptune

4. (C) – This planet has known life on it… A. Mars, B. Mercury, C. Earth, D. Venus

5. (B) – These planets have rings A. Earth and Mars, B. Neptune and Saturn, C. Mars and Mercury, D. Saturn and Earth

6. (D) – What is the great red spot on Jupiter? – A. fireball, B. hot spot, C. landing pad, D. hurricane-like storm

7. (B) – 70% of Earth's surface is covered by? – A. dirt, B. water, C. ants, D. magnetism

8. (C) – Why is Mars the "red planet"? – A. red clouds, B. red seas, C. iron dirt, D. apple orchards

9. (A) – The rings of Saturn are – A. ice and dust, B. gold and silver, C. imaginary, D. an optical illusion

10. (B) – The farthest planet from the sun is – A. Jupiter, B. Neptune, C. Saturn, D. Earth

Information source:
http://starchild.gsfc.nasa.gov/docs/StarChild/StarChild.html

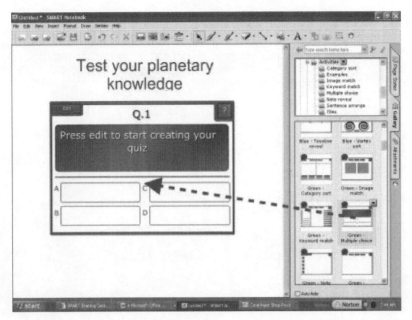

To begin your multiple choice activity, start with a new, blank Notebook software file (File->New), then click on the Gallery Tab, click the + in front of the Lesson Activity Toolkit folder, and scroll down to the Activities folder. Click on the Activities folder, and in the Search Results box, scroll down until you find the green Multiple Choice object, as shown above.

Drag the Multiple Choice object into the Whiteboarding area. Enter other text as you desire. Click on the green Edit button on the upper left corner of the Multiple Choice object and enter the questions and answers.

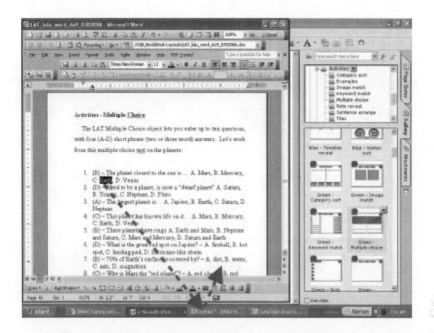

If you have prepared questions in a word processor and are using a Windows OS computer, there is an advanced method of question entry. Left click and drag to select the text when it is highlighted, then left click again and grab the selected text and drag to the to the Notebook software tab in the Windows taskbar. Keep your left mouse button held down and wait for Notebook software to open. Then continue holding your mouse button down and drag to the location in the Multiple Choice activity where you want to insert the text.

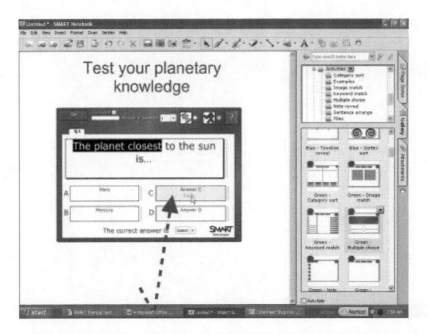

Above, you see the word "Earth" faintly showing under Answer C, signaling us that we correctly entered the word processing text using the click-and-drag method. Set the correct answer by clicking on the Select popup box, and dragging to A, B, C or D.

Question one is now complete. At the top of the screen, you can click on the radio button to the right of two choices for reinforcers (Well Done-Try Again) (green check-red X).

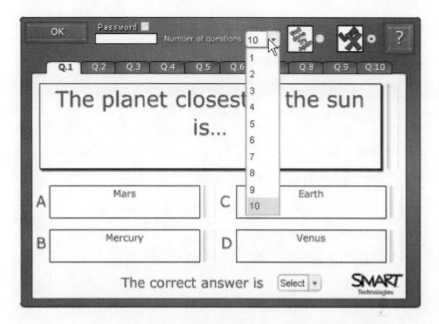

To enter the next question, use the Number of Questions pull down menu to choose the number of questions you want. You can choose up to ten.

When you are finished, click the OK button in the upper left corner, lock the object into place, and your multiple choice activity is ready for students to use. Remember to save your work.

You do not have to have a SMART Board interactive whiteboard attached to your computer to create or run Notebook software files using LAT objects. You just need to have Notebook software installed on your computer. You can create LAT curricular modules on your laptop even while sitting on the beach enjoying your favorite beverage (ha!). Students can replay your Notebook software files in the school's computer lab, as long as the lab computers have Notebook software installed.

Activities - Note Reveal

The LAT Note Reveal object lets you enter five important review points. Used like a "Family Feud" game, without scoring, Note Reveal adds interest to your lecture review.

Using the same method you used to drag other LAT objects out of the Gallery, drag the purple (or red, green, gold or blue) Note Reveal object to the Notebook software Whiteboarding area.

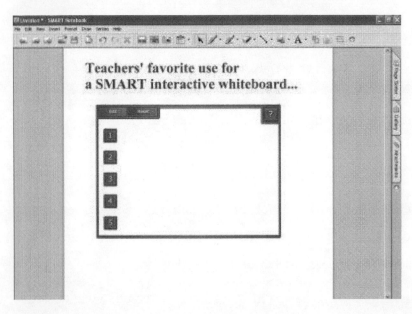

Enter a topic statement as the text of your five points. Tip: list the points from most important to least important, then click on point 5, and go UP to point 1.

On the next page, we have inserted five favorite uses for the SMART Board interactive whiteboard interactive whiteboard.

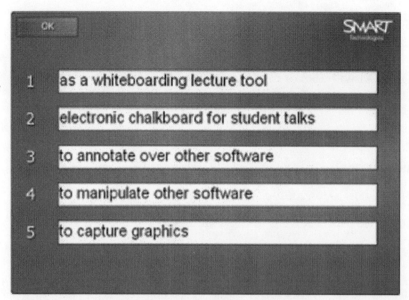

When you click on the Edit button on the upper left corner, you are able to edit the five points. Click OK to exit the edit mode.

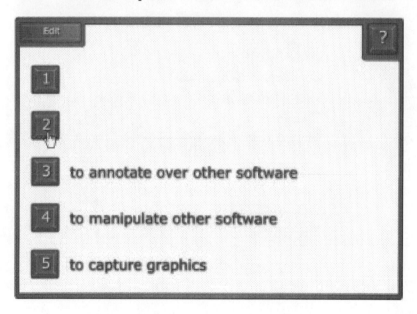

The above image shows what happens when you click on the numbers. Each point is revealed, reinforcing the most important concepts in your lecture.

You might like the Note Reveal you created so much, that you want to save it in the Gallery as a Notebook software page. Doing so will let you reuse it with lots of different Notebook software files, without retyping the content again.

You can use this advanced Notebook software feature to save any LAT activity you have created into the Gallery. Click on the Page Sorter tab. Then touch on the Notebook software page you have created (named Note_Reveal in this example). Hold down on the drop-down object menu and drag to Add Page to Gallery.

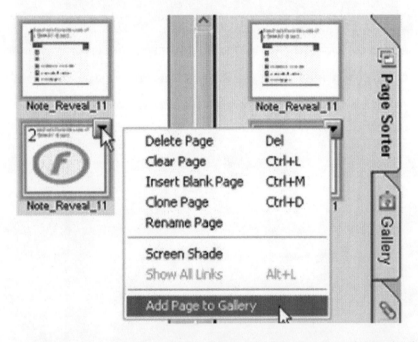

The page will be pasted into the main My Content folder in the Gallery. Now, you can insert this Notebook software page into any Notebook software file you create, at any time in the future.

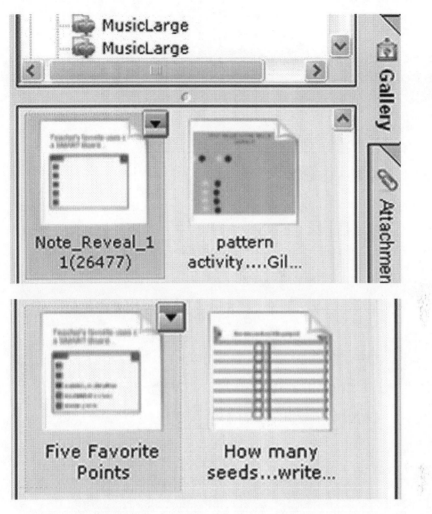

You can double click on the file name and rename it. Above, the Gallery-saved Notebook software page has been renamed "Five Favorite Points." Then, hold down on the drop-down object menu and drag to Properties. Your Note Reveal activity is finished and saved.

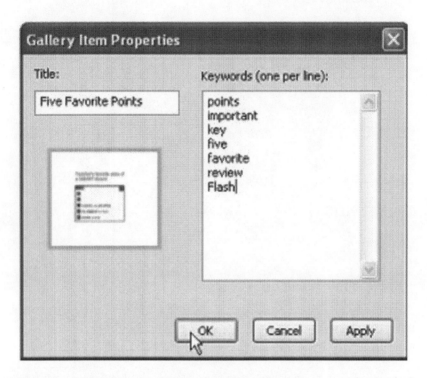

In the Gallery Item Properties menu, type in search keywords, so when you want to search for this Gallery object, you can use these terms to retrieve this object.

Type in Flash, so when you search for all Flash animation, this Gallery object comes up, too. Click OK to accept your changes.

Activities - Sentence Arrange

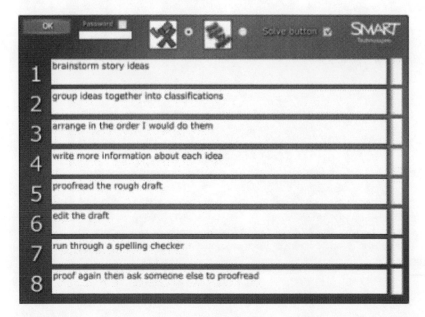

Above, we have used Sentence Arrange to sequence the steps one would take to write a paper. Drag the Sentence Arrange object onto the Notebook software Whiteboarding area from the Lesson Activity Toolkit Activities folder. Type the steps into Sentence Arrange, click OK and save the Notebook software file.

Use Sentence Arrange to help students sequence a story, understand the steps of an experiment, alphabetize spelling words, or even to prioritize events in a social studies cause-and-effect lecture.

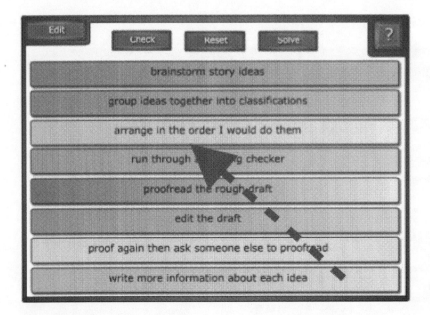

To scramble the order, click on the Reset button. Then drag the rectangles into proper sequence. Here, the first three steps of "writing a paper" are in the correct order, so you should click and drag on the last rectangle, to insert it as the fourth step.

Click the Check button to check your students' work. If your students are stumped, click Solve and the correct sequence will appear.

Activities – Tiles

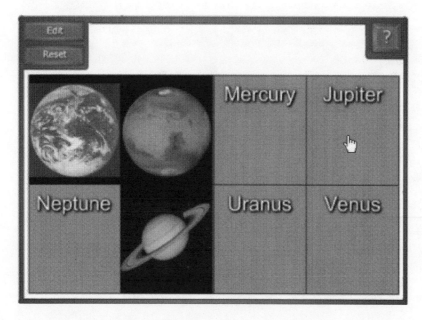

When you click on labeled tiles, graphics are revealed for learning review. Drag the Tiles object out of the Gallery LAT Activities folder.

You can have a different picture behind each tile, or single picture so each tile reveals a small part of the image.

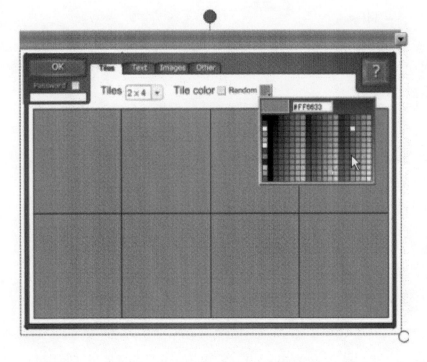

The next step in creating the Tiles activity is to click on the Edit button to change the Tile. Pull down on the tile matrix, as shown above, to choose the matrix you want. In this example you are seeing a 2x4 matrix.

Uncheck the Random Color box and click and hold on the color to select the color palette. We selected orange tiles to contrast with white text.

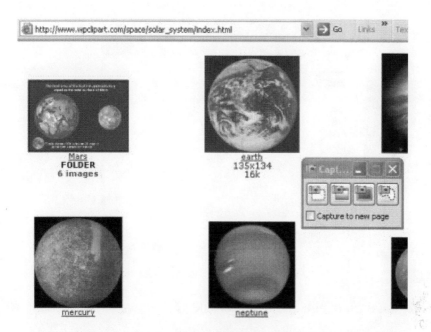

We are going to use the images above to create our Tiles activity. These images are available at the public domain graphics site www.wpclipart.com. First, activate the Screen Capture Tool in Notebook software, then go to wpclipart.com and capture each planet image.

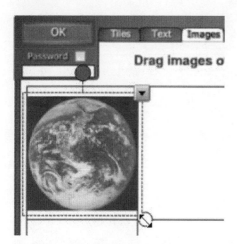

In Notebook software, position and resize each image so it fills either the width or height of a tile.

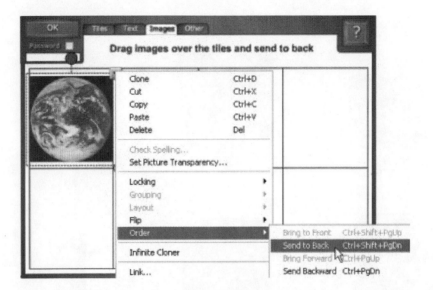

Click on each image, then click on the drop-down object menu (triangle on upper right corner of the selected image, shown above) and drag down to Order->Send to Back. Repeat for the rest of the planets.

When the planets are positioned, there will be some white space, so get the Notebook software Object tool (the square, triangle and circle icon), create a black rectangle with black border and draw the rectangle over the entire 2x4 tile area. Send this black rectangle to the back. (We used black because each planet background is black and everything will blend in.)

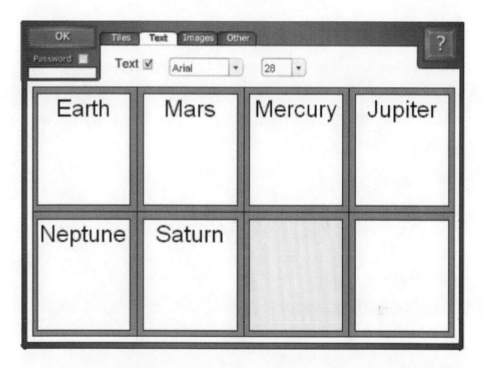

Select the Text tab and select the font and size you want to use (Arial 28). Type each planet name into each box. Here the 7th box is selected (it is yellow, when you are doing this on the computer). You can tab using your keyboard or click on a tile with your mouse to move from tile to tile. When you are finished, click the OK button on the upper left of the Tiles object, save your Notebook software file and you are ready to review the planets.

Using the Other tab, you can make the images selectable when you click on a tile, so an object could be an infinite clone object or a sound could be attached for replay. The Answer checkbox lets you enter an answer. The student then has to type in the answer to solve the puzzle. You can also change tile selection to manual, causing tiles to be randomly uncovered. Students then guess the hidden larger picture that is being revealed.

Activities - Timeline Reveal

Timeline Reveal is a great way to show a sequence of events. It is very useful for social studies. Below, we will create a Timeline Reveal, using names and dates of states that joined the United States after the Civil War.

1867 – Nebraska

1876 - Colorado

1889 – North Dakota, South Dakota, Montana, Washington

1890 – Idaho, Wyoming

1896 – Utah

1907 – Oklahoma

1912 – New Mexico, Arizona

1959 – Alaska, Hawaii

Source: http://www.enchantedlearning.com/usa/states/statehood.shtml

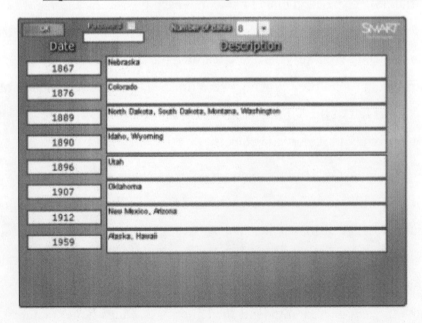

To create a Timeline Reveal using these eight dates, drag the orange Timeline Reveal object out of the LAT Activities area of the Gallery. Using the data on the previous page, click on the Edit button on the upper left corner. Click on the "Number of Dates" pull down and select 8. Type the dates and state names into the Timeline Reveal object.

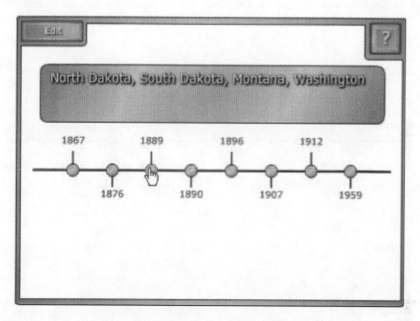

Save your work. Click OK to view the Timeline. To display the data for any particular date, click on the date in the timeline.

The Timeline Reveal is somewhat limited, because you cannot enter a month AND year, or a date like 10/12/1956. It also will not sort by date or scale dates.

Activities - Vortex Sort

The Vortex Sort is a fun way to have students sort words into two categories. In this example, we will use the 25 most popular words in the English language to create a Vortex Sort to quiz students on nouns, pronouns and verbs.

Here, the Vortex Labels will be "noun & pronoun" and "verb."

25 most popular English words (rank - type)

1 - you - pronoun

2 - I – noun

3 - to – preposition

4 - the - definitive article

5 - a - indefinite article, noun (the letter a)

6 - and – conjunction

7 - that - pronoun, adverb, conjunction, idiom

8 - it – pronoun

9 - of – preposition

10 - me – pronoun

11 - what - pronoun

12 - is – verb

13 - in – preposition

14 - this - pronoun, adjective

15 - know - verb

16 - I'm - contraction

17 - for - preposition

18 - no - adverb, adjective

19 - have - verb

20 - my - pronoun

21 – don't - contraction, verb

22 - just - adjective

23 - not - adverb

24 - do - verb

25 - be - verb

sources:
http://en.wiktionary.org/wiki/Wiktionary:Frequency_lists/TV/2006/1-1000

http://dictionary.reference.com

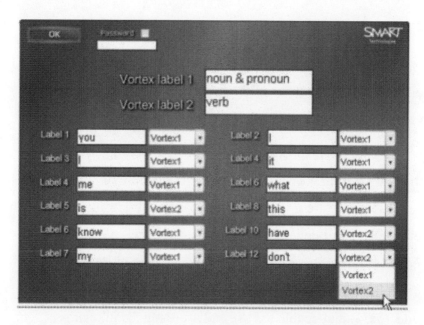

Enter the two vortex labels, then enter each label and identify which vortex each word belongs to. Save your Notebook software file.

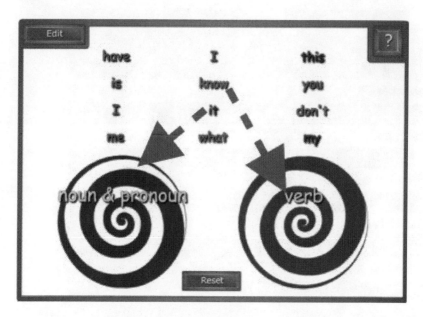

Pull each word to the correct vortex. Reset to rescramble words.

Games – Anagrams

Anagrams are a form of word play going back to ancient Greece and Rome. Anagrams can stimulate spatial centers of the brain, and can be a useful tool to help students improve spelling.

Spelling expert David Barnsdale researched spelling errors made in Internet newsgroup posts to develop a list of commonly misspelled words. These words are misspelled more than a third of the time: minuscule (68%), millennium (57%), embarrassment (55%), superseded (44%), occurrence (44%), accommodate (40%), accommodation (39%) occurring (37%), perseverance (36%), supersede (35%), noticeable (35%), embarrassing (35%), harass 34%), inoculate (34%).

source: http://www.barnsdle.demon.co.uk/spell/error.html

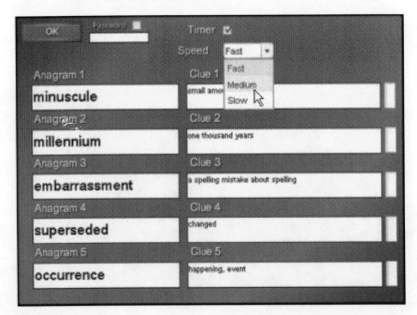

To create an anagram using these words, drag Anagrams from the LAT Games folder into Notebook software. Click on Edit to enter up to five spelling words and clues. Choose the speed at which you want students to work. To allow students to work without timed practice, click off the Timer checkbox. Enter a password if desired, click OK and save your work.

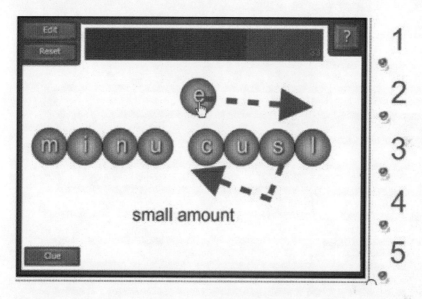

You can add sounds for each word for auditory reinforcement, if desired, by recording sounds using Audacity software and a simple computer microphone. Embed those saved audio files into Notebook software and link the sound files to objects (like the numbers 1-5 shown above). In this example, a student clicks on the sound icon next to each number.

Audacity is wonderful FREE sound recording software, available at: http://audacity.sourceforge.net.

Games – Crossword

Arthur Wynne created the first "word-cross" puzzle for the New York World newspaper in 1913 and crossword puzzles have been popular since. Crossword puzzles are great tools to help students link vocabulary words to definitions.

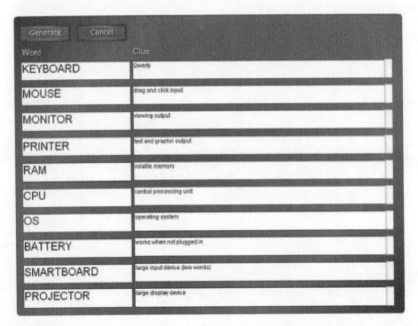

To create a Crossword Activity, drag Crossword from the LAT Games folder into Notebook software. Click on Edit to enter up to ten words and clues. Then, click Generate and once your puzzle is generated, save your work. If the puzzle cannot be generated, the Crossword object will give you a warning.

In the example, above and on the next page, we are creating a crossword puzzle to review computer terms.

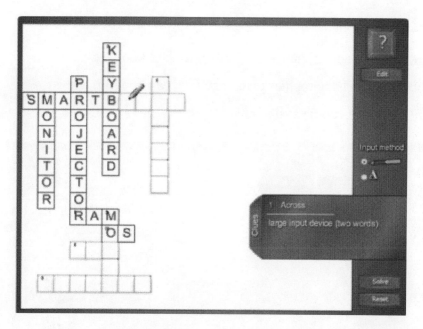

When you are using Crossword with students, have them click on the Clues tab first, then click on the tiles they want the clue for.

Students can input answers using either a keyboard or the SMART Board interactive whiteboard stylus. Research shows that the handwriting of students (especially boys) improves with regular use of an interactive whiteboard. Crossword is a fun way to give students practice printing as well as building vocabulary and spelling skills.

Games – Hot Spots

Hot Spots is one of the LAT's most powerful knowledge reinforcement tools. Graphics on any subject can be used, and identifying points can be easily added.

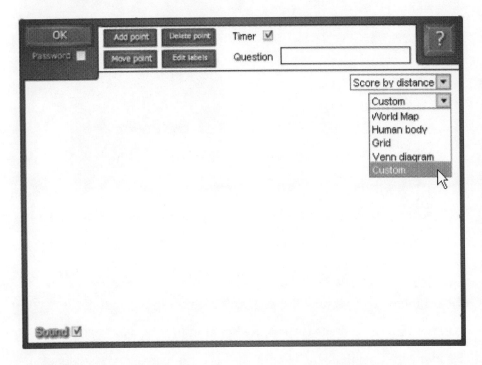

Drag the Hot Spots object out of the LAT Games Gallery and into Notebook software. Click the Edit button and change the background to Custom.

You will want to create a graphic clip that has an aspect ratio of 1.65:1. Our favorite Windows graphic software is Corel Paint Shop Pro, which lets you take a screen capture, then clip it to the pixel size or aspect ratio you want. Alternatively, use the Screen Capture tool and keep clipping it until you get it to size, or size it as close as possible to the Hot Spots viewing area.

Save your graphic, then insert the picture into Notebook software

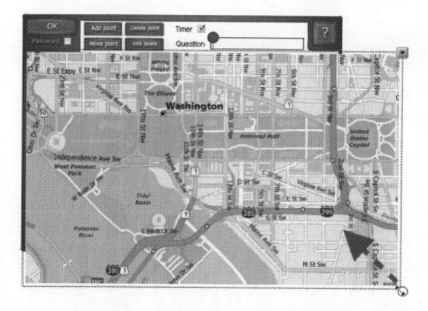

This Washington DC map was pasted into Notebook software and repositioned so the upper left corner fits in the Hot Spot viewing window. It is being resized (below) by dragging on the Resize handle on the lower right corner of the image.

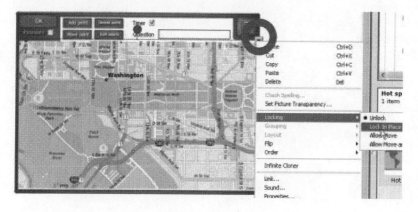

Once the image is resized, click on the drop-down object menu (the triangle on upper right of the image), choose Locking->Lock in Place.

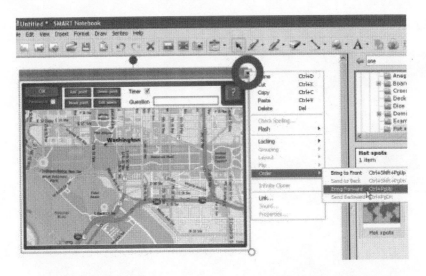

Then click on the Hot Spot object frame to select it (above), pull the drop-down object menu (triangle on upper right of the image) and choose Order->Bring Forward, then Locking->Lock in Place.

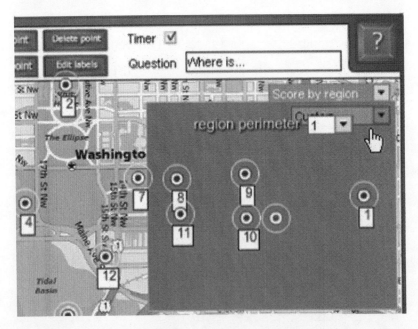

Click on the Add Point button to add your Hot Spot points. Label each point, enter the question ("Where is…"), set the region perimeter to see how far away from the target someone can be and still be right.

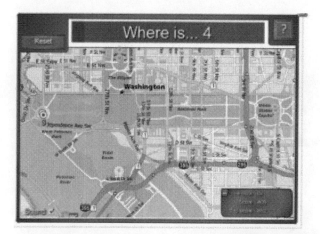

1 - U.S. Capitol
2 - White House
3 - Lincoln Memorial
4 - Washington Monument
5 - Vietnam Vet Memorial
6 - Jefferson Memorial

7 - National Museum of American History
8 - National Museum of Natural History
9 - National Gallery of Art
10 - National Air and Space Museum
11 - Smithsonian Institute
12 - Bureau of Printing and Engraving
13 - Reflecting Pool

This is what the completed Hot Spot looks like after the student clicks on the Start button in the upper left corner. The question / timer runs in the red bar at the top center of the Hot Spot object. The mouse turns into a red and bullseye (currently on left side of page at the Lincoln Memorial).

Although the Hot Spot is the most complex LAT tool to use, it is very graphically versatile and a favorite among teachers and students.

Games – Sudoku

This wildly popular number-logic game was first invented by
American architect Howard Garns in 1979, under the title "Number
Place." This is a very popular game in Japan.

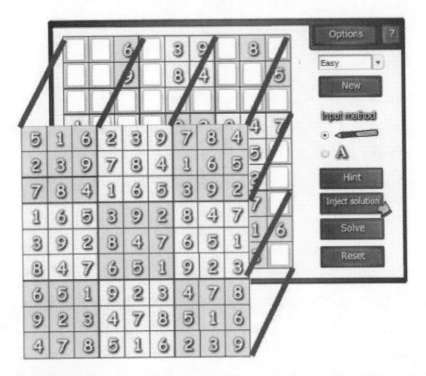

Just drag the LAT Sudoku out of the Gallery and start to fill in
blanks with numbers. Set options for different difficulty levels. When
you click on Hint, the Sudoku object fills one of the numbers into a
Sudoku square. Click on the Inject Solution button to see the solution.
You can work the puzzle using either the keyboard or the SMART
Board interactive whiteboard stylus.

When you are stumped, you can click the Solve button (as shown
here) to see the finished Sudoku puzzle.

Games – Word Biz

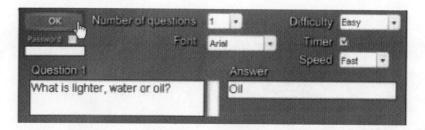

Word Play lets you enter up to eight spelling or simple facts into Word Biz, for a fun review and practice. Click "Edit" and enter up to five question clues and their answers. Click OK when finished and save your work.

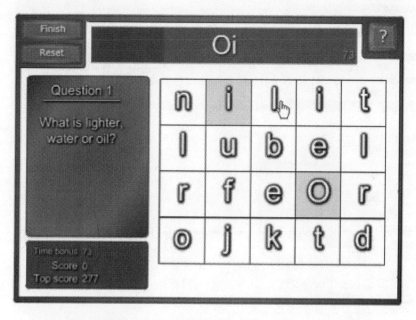

Click on Start, then click on the tiles to spell out the word for each question you created, as shown above. Rotate Word Biz with other LAT Activities and Games for some variety in spelling drill and practice.

Games – Word Guess

Students can play Word Guess on the SMART Board interactive whiteboard or computers as a twist on the old "hangman" game.

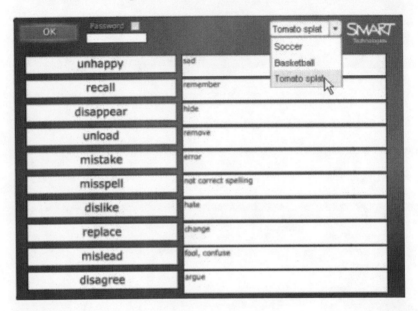

Enter up to ten spelling words and definitions into Word Guess.

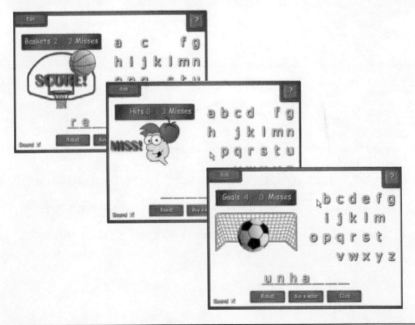

Lesson Activity Toolkit

Tools – Balloon Pop

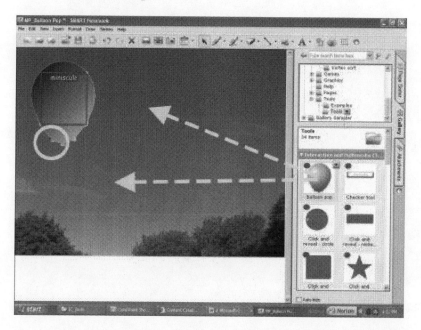

Use Balloon Pop for a fun and colorful vocabulary review. Pull Balloon Pop out of the LAT Tools. We've taken our own pictures of a blue sky with a digital camera and inserted it into Notebook software (Insert->Picture File). You might go onto the school playground and take some scenic shots of your school building, to "fly" balloons over.

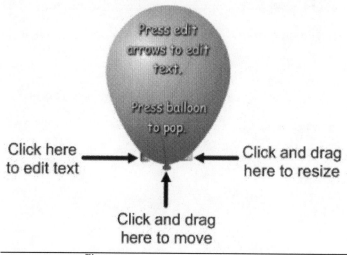

Once you have created your balloon pop review, save it and then display it in Notebook software full screen so it is easy to see. There is some animation when each balloon pops. Although the balloon words are hard to read in the picture above, they are much easier to see when projected on an interactive whiteboard.

You can also create balloon pages without text and save your work. Then, when you are ready, copy and paste words into your Notebook software file, and drag the words right into the balloons to enter text.

You can also use the balloon as a reveal, typing the words onto a Notebook software page, adding balloons, typing a small definition into the balloon and saving. Students pop the balloon "definitions" to reveal the review word.

Tools – Checker Tool

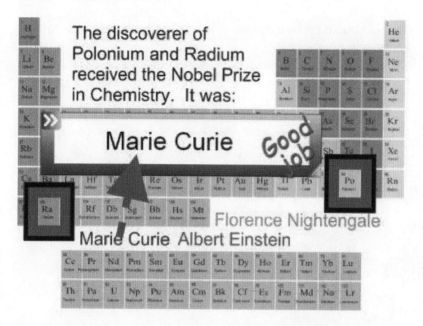

Drag the Checker Tool into your Notebook software file from the LAT Tools folder. Create some text answers in Notebook software, then drag the text into the spaces shown.

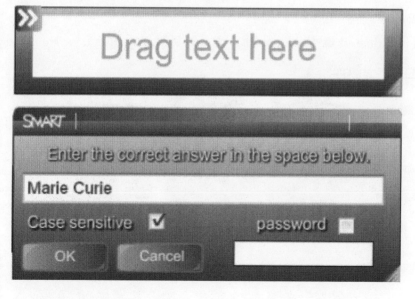

Then enter the correct answer. Very easy to do!!!

Tools – Dice–Image

It is easy to make picture dice to reinforce graphic images or just have some fun. Drag the Dice-Image LAT Tool into Notebook software's Whiteboarding area. Insert six fairly square JPEG images.

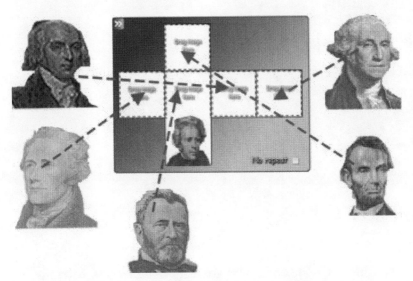

Open up the Dice-image (click on the chevrons on the upper left corner). Drag each image onto a die face. Click the No Repeat box if desired and then close the Dice-image tool. (Image source: http://www.bep.treas.gov)

To roll your die, click on it. You can resize the die by pulling its light blue resize handle, located on the lower right corner of the die.

Save your new die by dragging it into the My Content folder of the Gallery. You can share this die with others by clicking on the drop-down object menu (triangle) of the die you just created, and Export as Collection File.

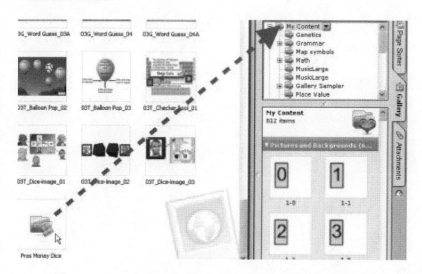

You can easily email your export file to other teachers. They can save it to a folder on their computer and drag it into the "My Content" folder on their computer. Another interesting and fun use of this activity is to create dice with pictures of your students and using them to randomly choose students to call on.

Tools – Dice – Keyword

The keyword dice works much like the image dice activity. Drag the Dice-keyword from the LAT Tools and click on the Open chevrons in the upper left corner. Type in the words you want to reinforce, and click the chevrons closed.

Click on the die to shake.

Tools – Question Flipper

Teachers often use the Question Flipper to create a Jeopardy!™ game in Notebook software. TV Guide has rated Jeopardy!™ as #2 most popular game show ever. It is great for learning reinforcement.

Enter a question and answer on opposite sides of the Question Flipper LAT Tool. Click the blue and white Open chevrons on the upper left corner of the tool to edit. On the Front side, we typed in "Who was President for four terms of office?" and changed the font to 24 point, Arial, yellow text, blue background. The Back side "Franklin D. Roosevelt" is 26 point, Arial, white text, red background.

When you click on the tile, the answer is revealed.

This is a similar Question Flipper – 2 Tool.

Tools – Question Flipper–Image

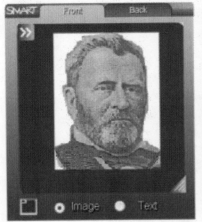 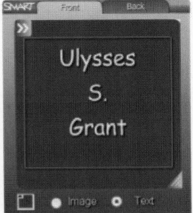

The Question Flipper–Image Tool works much the same way, but allows you to paste a JPEG image onto the flipping tile. An easy way to do this is to use the Screen Capture tool to clip images which will be instantly pasted into Notebook software. From there, you can pull them as images onto the Question Flipper.

To edit, click on the text or image radio buttons at the bottom of the tool. You can change either side of the tile's background color.

To access each side of the tile, click on the Front and Back tabs, located at the top of the tool.

Tools – Random Image Tool

This can be a useful tool if you have a lot of graphics in a lesson and want to provide a random drill.

You can fill the Random Image Tool with different graphics, including these Gallery graphics (above).

To add another image, click the Add button to get the "Drag Image Here" directions. Then drag in your image.

When you are finished, click the Edit area closed and save your work. You may want to drag this tool to My Gallery for quick access. Click on the center of the Random Image Tool to generate a graphic. Click on the yellow Inject Arrow (lower left corner) to inject a copy of the image to the Notebook software Whiteboarding area.

The injected image is smaller than the original image. You can resize it if you wish, by clicking on it and pulling the resize handle. The Random Image tool has to be moved around the screen, so there is room to inject each image.

Something we don't like about the Random Image Tool is that graphics WITH sound that are dragged into the Random Image Tool DO NOT retain their sound files.

For fun, consider creating a Random Image Tool with pictures of all your students, and use randomly to choose who to call on.

Tools – Random Number and Letter Generators

The Random Number Generator injects numeric values, based on the range you specify when you open up the Flash object.

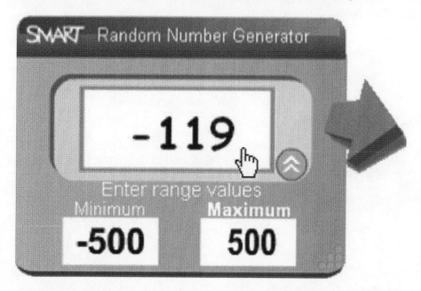

Click on the box in the center of the Random Number Generator to generate a value. Then click on the inject arrow. The number is injected into the Notebook software Whiteboarding area.

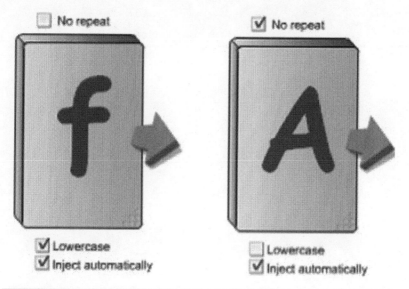

Random Letter and Vowel tools work great. Clicking on the "Inject automatically" check box causes the letter to be injected just by clicking on the tile. The tile rotates, the letter appears in the tile, and it is injected into Notebook software.

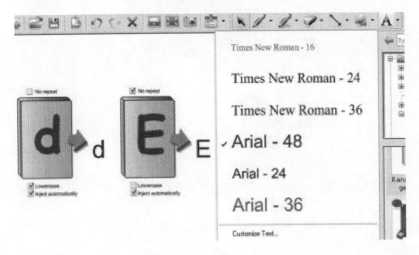

Set the text attributes (font, size, and color) by selecting the font tool in the Notebook software tools pull down menu. If you have Notebook software 10, you can also use the new Properties Tab in the Special Area.

Tools – Scrolling Text Banner

Use the Scrolling Text Banner to add visual interest to your Notebook file.

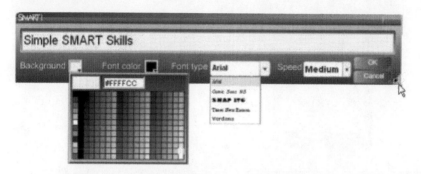

Pull the Scrolling Text Banner out of the Gallery LAT Tools area and double click on it. You are now in the edit mode and can now enter text, change the background and font color, select among five font types, alter the speed (slow, medium, fast) and resize the banner.

The banner looks like this, with the red arrows indicating motion. With the pointer tool selected, you can grab the banner and move it. You can also select and right click on it to adjust properties, such as locking it into place. If you want to resize the banner, say, to fill the Whiteboarding area, you must resize it in the edit mode.

Tools – Text Splitter

Use the Text Splitter for sentence diagramming.

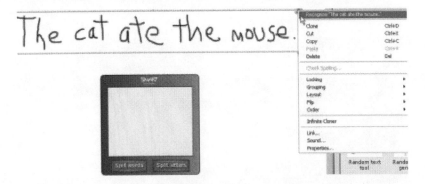

    The Text Splitter Tool is in the LAT Gallery Tools section. Have a student write a sentence on the board. Convert the handwriting to text using Notebook software's handwriting recognition features (click on the handwriting and use the object pull-down menu to choose the best handwriting recognition "guess." Edit with the virtual keyboard if needed.

Drag the converted handwriting into the Text Splitter tool.

The sentence is automatically entered into the Text Splitter tool. Click on the "Split words" button to inject the individual words into the Notebook software Whiteboarding area. They will be created with the font attributes you have previously selected in the Text Tool pull down menu (or in the Notebook software 10 Properties tab).

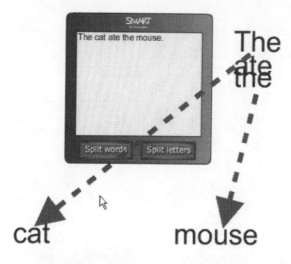

Move text objects around the Notebook software page as you desire, and use Notebook software to enhance your words.

Tools – Vote Tool

The Vote Tool can be used to poll your students on any question you like. Just write or type the choices on the SMART Board interactive whiteboard, and add Vote Tools from the LAT.

Above, two Vote Tools have been pulled from the LAT Tools folder to create this lunch voting tool to give the teacher a lunch count. When each student clicks on the arrow to vote, the arrow outline turns red and the count is incremeted.

Tools – Word Generator

Word Generator is a great tool to review spelling words.

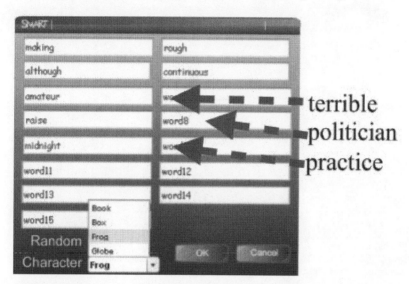

In this example, we will use a list of ten frequently misspelled words: making, although, raise, amateur, midnight, rough, terrible, continuous, politician, practice.

Drag the Word Generator from the Gallery LAT Tools into the Whiteboarding area. To enter words into the word list, click on the blue Reset button on the lower left corner of Word Generator,

Click in each box for word entry then type in your words. Alternatively, drag words in which you typed (or wrote and used Handwriting Recognition) in Notebook software. Here we typed in ten commonly misspelled words. Enter blanks for words you do not use (word11…word15).

In the lower left corner, change the character from Frog to Box, using the popup menu. Then click on the OK button.

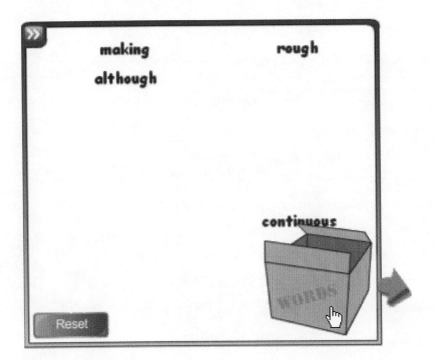

Every time you click on the box, one of the review words floats out of the book. Click on the inject arrow to inject the words into the Whiteboarding area.

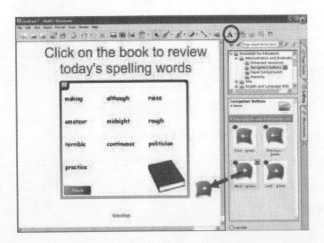

Add simple directions to your page by clicking on the Text Tool (A), then clicking in the top center of the screen. Type in the directions and change the text properties (we used 48 point, Arial font, center justified). Resize and move the text box around as desired.

In the Gallery, go to the Essentials for Educators folder. Click on the + in front of the folder, then click on the + in front of the Administration and Evaluation subfolder, and click on the Navigation buttons folder. Pull the Next – Green button onto the page and resize it (click on the lower right corner and pull to the center of the button)

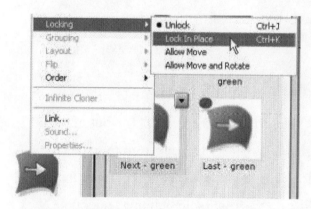

Finally, right click (use the Virtual Right Mouse Button on the Pen Tray) on each object (the red text, the Word Generator, and the green next arrow), and drag up to Locking->Lock In Place.

Graphics - Pull Tab

Use Pull Tabs to put information off to the side in Notebook software. Reveal by pulling the Pull Tab, as desired.

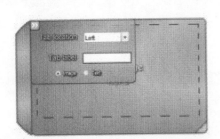
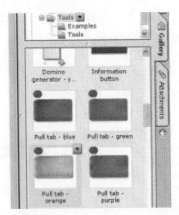

To set up this Pull Tab activity, drag the Pull Tab out of the Gallery LAT Tools area. Click on the two chevrons to open it. Choose your tab location (left, right, top or bottom). Enter the tab label "Directions." Click on the Text radio button, then double click on the text (or select and drag to highlight), and enter text.

1 - U.S. Capitol
2 - White House
3 - Lincoln Memorial
4 - Washington Monument
5 - Vietnam Vet Memorial
6 - Jefferson Memorial

7 - National Museum of American History
8 - National Museum of Natural History
9 - National Gallery of Art
10 - National Air and Space Museum
11 - Smithsonian Institute
12 - Bureau of Printing and Engraving
13 - Reflecting Pool

Here is a completed Directions Pull Tab in the Washington DC Hot Spots created earlier in <u>Simple SMART™ Skills</u>. The Directions Tab is on the right edge of the screen, with the tab facing left.

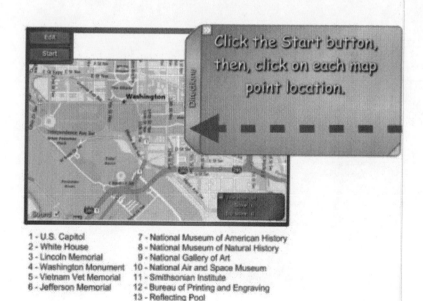

1 - U.S. Capitol
2 - White House
3 - Lincoln Memorial
4 - Washington Monument
5 - Vietnam Vet Memorial
6 - Jefferson Memorial

7 - National Museum of American History
8 - National Museum of Natural History
9 - National Gallery of Art
10 - National Air and Space Museum
11 - Smithsonian Institute
12 - Bureau of Printing and Engraving
13 - Reflecting Pool

4

www.smarttech.com

In this chapter we are going to explore Support, Training and Education at www.smarttech.com.

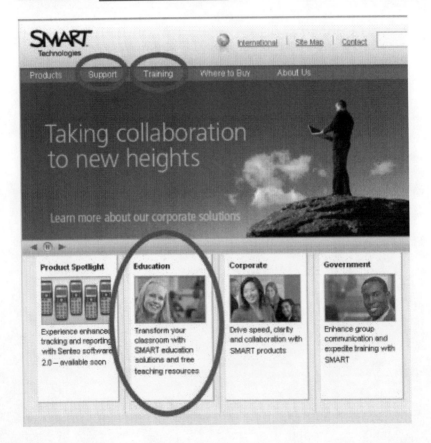

In the Support section, you can download the current version of Notebook software and other software, such as Essentials for Educators. Click on SMART Notebook software (circled above) to access the download area and other support documents.

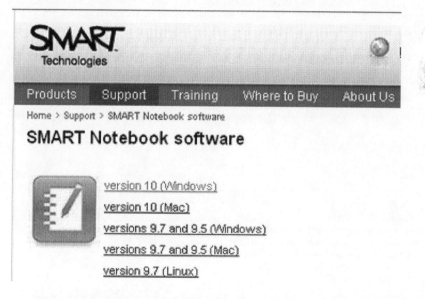

Click on the version and operating system you want to download.

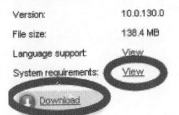

Click the **Download** button to download version 10 on your computer. Follow the on-screen instructions.

Download details

Version:	10.0.130.0
File size:	138.4 MB
Language support:	View
System requirements:	View

Download

If you have never installed SMART software on your computer (or if you have uninstalled <u>all</u> SMART software) you can install the latest version of Notebook software on your computer. (If you have a Senteo™ interactive response system, read the website directions on proper installation).

The easiest way to install Notebook software 10 is to install the 30-day trial version first. After installation, activate it with a software licensing key. Get the licensing key from your I.T. administrator, or via www.smarttech.com with the serial number from your SMART™ product.

Click on "View" to see the computer hardware and software you need to run this version of Notebook software. For Windows machines:

Pentium II 450 MHz processor
256 MB of RAM (512 MB recommended)
180 MB of free hard disk space for minimum installation (840 MB for full installation with Gallery collections)
Windows 2000, Windows XP or Windows Vista operating system
Internet Explorer internet browser 6.0 or later
Adobe Flash player version 8

Requirements for SMART Video Player
Pentium II 450 MHz processor (700 MHz or faster recommended)
Windows 2000 operating system or later
Microsoft DirectX technology 8.1 or later

Macintosh requirements for Notebook software 10:

700 MHz processor (1 GHz or faster recommended) PowerPC G3, G4 or G5
processors and Intel processors (universal binary)
256 MB of RAM (512 MB recommended)
85 MB of free hard disk space for minimum installation (825 MB for full
installation with Gallery collections)
Mac OS X version 10.4.x operating system software or later (does not
support Mac OS X version 10.5.3)
Safari application program version 1.3.2 or later

If you have an older computer or operating system, you will need to use a previous version of Notebook software. We have a non-Intel Power PC Macintosh. We can run Notebook software 10 using Tiger 10.4.x operating system or Notebook software 9.7 using Leopard 10.5.x operating system. But program issues in Macintosh Notebook software 10 require that it run on Intel processors (for Macintosh) only.

If in doubt, you can call SMART Technical Support, 1-888-42-SMART (also 866-518-6791), weekdays, 6 A.M. to 6 P.M, Central Time. When the phone menu prompts you, choose Technical Support, thenSoftware Support. You do not even need a SMART product serial number to make a FREE technical support call to SMART.

If you want to run the SMART Lesson Activity Toolkit, we recommend Notebook software 9.7 or higher for Windows, and Notebook software 10 for Macintosh. It is possible to run LAT on Notebook software 9.7 Macintosh, but the Flash animations can perform in unexpected ways. To get the current Flash player, download it at www.adobe.com.

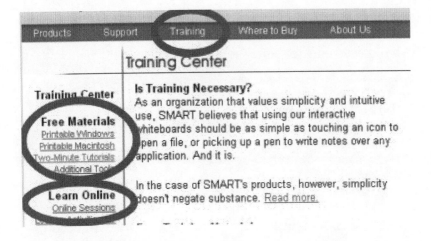

There is a wealth of FREE training on SMART's website, including Two Minute Tutorials (two minute streaming videos to teach you about different aspects of SMART Board interactive whiteboard use), Printed Windows and Macintosh materials (downloadable Quick Reference guides, usually 2-3 pages long), and access to SMART's free Online Sessions (30-45 minute web conferences you can attend).

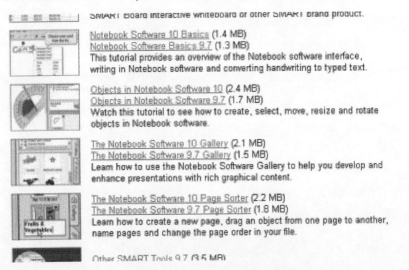

All you need to access Two Minute Tutorials is a high speed Internet connection, a computer and computer speakers. Click on a link to view a Two Minute Tutorial. This free training is great.

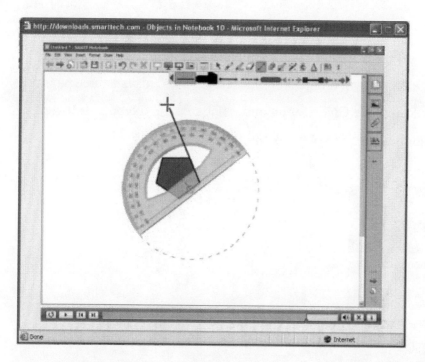

In the Two Minute Tutorial, Objects in Notebook software 10 (above), you will quickly learn how to create a Shape (pentagon) in Notebook software, change its color, drag an object (protractor) out of Notebook software Gallery, resize and rotate it, and extend one side of the pentagon with a line, so you can measure the pentagon's angle.

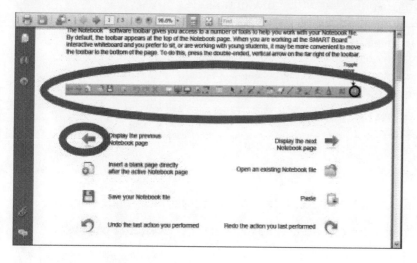

Simple SMART™ Skills

In the Printed Windows and Printed Macintosh section of Training/Free Materials, we downloaded the Notebook software 10 Tools PDF (shown on the bottom of page 97). This is a three page Quick Reference Guide for an important area of Notebook software, commonly used for Notebook training sessions.

Education

Transform your classroom with SMART education solutions and free teaching resources

To learn more about curricular materials that work with your SMART Board interactive whiteboard, visit www.smarttech.com, click on the Education section on the lower left corner to go to Educator resources and then to Community.

> **Online classroom resources**
> Browse this list of websites to find free, curriculum-related resources for your classroom.
> › Elementary
> › Secondary

Scroll to the bottom of the Educator Resources page to go to Online classroom resources, a list of great educational websites.

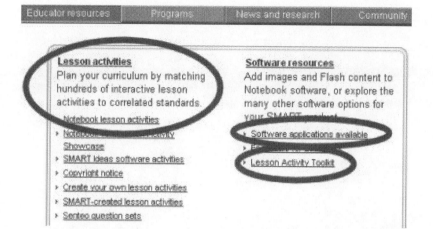

At the top of the Educator Resources page, you will also have access to almost a thousand prebuilt Notebook Lesson Activities that you can easily use and modify to fit your exact needs. You can also go to Software Applications Available to download SMART Speller and Number Cruncher for Windows, and Coda Finale Notepad for music composition for both Macintosh and Windows.

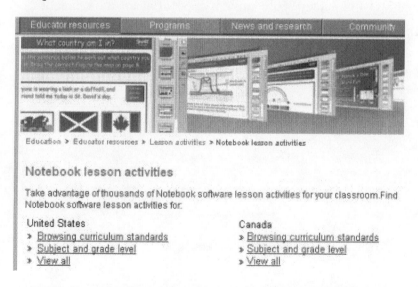

When looking for prebuilt Notebook software files, Educator Resources is a great place to start. Choose your country (if you are teaching modern languages, you might choose Europe or America Latina), then decide if you want to browse by curriculum standards, subject and grade level, or view all.

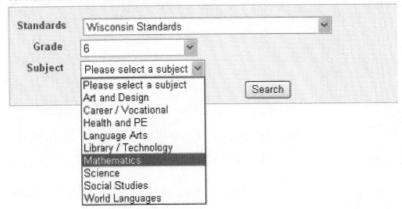

In this example, we chose Wisconsin Standards, Grade 6, Mathematics. Elementary core content areas offer the most prebuilt Notebook software content.

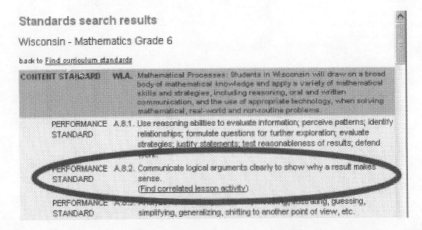

There is a correlated lesson activity for Wisconsin DPI standard A.8.2. Click on the blue link to "Find correlated lesson activity."

A.8.2. - Communicate logical arguments clearly to show why a result mal

Theoretical and Experimental Probability (Coins - US)

Understand the concepts of event, outcome, experiment, theoretical probability an
probability. Solve problems using the formula for probability and understand how ɪ
fairness of a game.

Theoretical and Experimental Probability (Dice)

Understand the concepts of event, outcome, experiment, theoretical probability an
probability. Solve problems using the formula for probability and understand how ɪ
fairness of a game.

Theoretical and Experimental Probability (Question Set)

Use Santeo interactive response system to test knowledge of the concept of ther

These three Notebook software files on SMART's Education website came up as being correlated to WI Math A.8.2. Click on any of the blue links to see more information.

Theoretical and Experimental Probability (Coins - US)

Understand the concepts of event,
outcome, experiment, theoretical
probability and experimental probability.
Solve problems using the formula for
probability and understand how probability
relates to the fairness of a game.

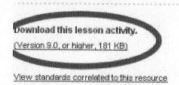

Download this lesson activity.
(Version 9.0, or higher, 181 KB)

View standards correlated to this resource

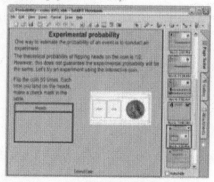

View larger image

Author:	Coralie Olesen
Country:	United States
Level:	Elementary
Grade:	4-6
Subject:	Math

A screen shot like the one above, gives us a good idea of the content in the file. Click on the download link to download it. Windows users can also right-click to "Save Target As..." as an alternate downloading method.

Simple SMART™ Skills

With the Notebook software file downloaded on your computer, you can open it up in Notebook software to preview for an upcoming lecture. If you have a good working knowledge of Notebook software tools, you can modify and adapt this Notebook software file as desired.

Warm and Cool Colors

Explore warm and cool colors in art.

- -

Download this lesson activity.

(Version 8.1.1, or higher, 2746 KB)

View standards correlated to this resource

- -

Author:	Joan Ba ger
Country:	United States
Level:	Elementary
Grade:	K-3
Subject:	Art and Design

Some of my favorite Notebook software files are written by one of about 400 SMART Exemplary Educators in North America. The best way to find these "classroom tested" Notebook software files is to "Search All." This will show you all files submitted to SMART in 2005 and 2006. Go to approximately page 15, at the bottom of the search list screen. A yellow star by the author tells you that a SMART Exemplary Educator created this Notebook software file.

You can do a Google search for additional Notebook software files, but one of the best new depositories of Notebook software files is the SMART Exchange http://exchange.smarttech.com/files.

The SMART Exchange is a bulletin board where teachers ask questions, share ideas and learn. The SMART Exchange also announces Notebook software file contests for teachers.

Other places for more information:

www.youtube.com – over 1,000 SMART Board interactive whiteboard movies

www.teachertube.com – over 100 SMART Board interactive whiteboard movies

http://smartboards.typepad.com – James Hollis' great Teachers Love SMART Board interactive whiteboards blog

5

Research

As shown empirically and through research, interactive whiteboards are indeed powerful educational tools. To date, the best research study available is ***Embedding ICT In The Literacy And Numeracy Strategies, Higgins, Steve (et.al), April, 2005*** from BECTA (the British Educational Communications and Technology Agency).

You can download the complete research report at:

http://partners.becta.org.uk/page_documents/research/univ_newcastle_evaluation_whiteboards.pdf

Highlights of the study are summarized below:

The pace of instruction increases 17% when interactive whiteboards are used in the classroom, so content gets covered more quickly. Math lessons, in particular, are faster paced.

Student interaction improves. Students provide more detailed answers to teacher questions when interactive whiteboards are used in instruction.

Interactive whiteboards increase teacher flexibility in lesson delivery and improve student motivation.

Seven out of eight teachers believe that using interactive whiteboards make them more confident using interactive computer technology.

Interactive whiteboards create a paradigm shift in teaching. Seventy percent of teachers using interactive whiteboards do more whole class instruction, and believe that using an interactive whiteboard has affected the structure of their language arts and mathematics sessions.

Ninety-nine percent of teachers feel that interactive whiteboard use increases student motivation. Four out of five teachers believe that boys are "more motivated, interested, focused, and participate more… Boys thoroughly enjoy the visual aspect and have improved their writing."

For girls, use of interactive whiteboards helps girls with spatial awareness. Girls tend to want to use the interactive whiteboard for drawing and artwork.

The report states that in pupil interviews "a word frequently used… is 'easier.' In this context it seems to refer to actually 'seeing' what the teacher is doing and combining what is seen with the teacher's explanation. The impression is, however, that 'seeing' first, aids understanding."

Multimedia elements appear to play a part in engaging pupils and holding their attention. Pupils report that they enjoy sounds, the visual aspects, and touching the interactive whiteboard.

Interactive whiteboards help learning by allowing students to touch the board and get instant feedback. If the answer is revealed with an accompanying positive sound, the learning experience is further enhanced.

The capacity to save work and return to it later is also valued by pupils. As one pupil stated, "you can bring up yesterday's work and be reminded of things when you are doing your story."

Most pupils believe that interactive whiteboards help them to pay better attention during the lessons. "It is colorful and gets your attention."

Most students like having their work shown on the interactive whiteboard... For most, it seems an opportunity to learn, to improve their work. Some said, "I like to show off a bit."

Using interactive whiteboards to save and print reduces the need for notetaking. This, in turn, allows students time to process information in more depth.

Interactive whiteboards help create greater interest in math. The real-time movement such as rotation alongside visual cues such as highlighting greatly facilitates the teaching of fractions, measurement of angles and a variety of transformation such as translation and tessellation.

Whole class game playing on an interactive whiteboard allows teachers to monitor pupils' progress and to identify weaknesses or misconceptions early so they can be rectified.

Interactive whiteboards increase presentation efficiency, by allowing the teacher instant access to material from a variety of sources and the possibility of using pre-prepared lessons that move without apparent effort from the visual to the verbal and back again.

Using interactive whiteboards quickens the pace of lessons. There is less time spent on "a preoccupation with management of resources" such as the real time throwing of dice in math lessons or the need to keep referring to one's teaching notes. Additionally, less time is spent on drawing as images are already available from the Notebook software Gallery.

Teachers report that there are time savings in planning and saving lessons. Although it can take time to prepare lessons with an interactive whiteboard, teachers report that planning time is eventually reduced. Many teachers believe that the extra time in preparing lessons is an "investment."

Interactive whiteboard lessons also help teachers face the class more, spending more time focusing on their pupils.

One of the main claims of using an interactive whiteboard as a pedagogic tool is that it promotes an "interactive" class. Research studies state that students are motivated in lessons… because of the "high level of interaction – students enjoy interacting physically with the board, manipulating text and images… and teachers consider the active participation of their students."

A very powerful activity utilizing class cohesiveness is a "whole-class modeling exercise" based on one pupil's piece of work, displayed and annotated over, using an interactive whiteboard. "This lecture approach widens the perception of audience for pupils' writing to more than just the teacher... providing the basis for class discussion and peer feedback."

The study concludes that interactive whiteboards are a transformative device when they become part of the regular fabric of classroom life. Teachers' development with interactive whiteboard use depends on easy and frequent access (i.e. in their own classrooms).

We hope this book gives you new ideas toward more confidently and creatively using the SMART Board interactive whiteboard in your own classroom. Using your interactive whiteboard regularly can help you take your teaching from good to <u>GREAT</u>!!!

We wish you and your students many wonderful learning opportunities in the future.

- Mike Palecek

Made in the USA
Lexington, KY
26 January 2010